SING THE
FAITH

Hymns of
LENT

PAUL WESTERMEYER

Augsburg Fortress
PUBLISHERS

SING THE FAITH

Hymns of
LENT

PAUL WESTERMEYER

Editors:
Gloria E. Bengtson,
Jeffrey S. Nelson, and
Sarah Anondson
Cover design:
Marti Naughton

Scripture quotations
are from New Revised
Standard Version
Bible, copyright
© 1989 Division of
Christian Education
of the National
Council of the
Churches of Christ in
the United States of
America. Used by
permission.

Copyright © 2003
Augsburg Fortress
All rights reserved.
May not be
reproduced.
ISBN 0-8066-4679-9
Manufactured
in U.S.A.

06 05 04 03 1 2 3 4

Introduction 3

The Glory of These Forty Days 7

By the Babylonian Rivers 15

Ah, Holy Jesus, How Have You Offended 23

O Sacred Head, Now Wounded 31

Sing, My Tongue 39

Resources 47

INTRODUCTION

Welcome to Sing the Faith!

Welcome to *Hymns of Lent,* one of nine volumes in the Sing the Faith Bible study series. You are embarking on a biblical exploration of grace through the poetry, music, and history of five of the most beloved hymns of the Christian tradition.

Hymns are the faith people sing. The lyrics are owned by the people as the fabric of their theology. Many hymns have been in the memories of churchgoers for years. The melodies and texts of hymns are often retained after most other memory has faded. This series will allow participants to connect these well-loved hymns to biblical texts.

Pastors and worship leaders spend a significant amount of time searching for hymns related to the Sunday readings, the theme, and the mood of each service. Indexes are available to assist planners in coordinating biblical texts and songs. The Sing the Faith series brings this information and its powerful faith formation capability to you.

Each session focuses on one hymn. Participants will reflect on their personal history with the hymn, explore biblical connections in the texts, learn the history and legends associated with the hymn, and consider how the message of the hymn applies to their daily journey of faith.

Preparing your study

The Sing the Faith series, designed for small-group Bible study, encourages interaction among participants to help them grow and enrich their journeys of faith. Alternate groupings, with minor modifications, would be possible. Individuals might use this resource for personal study or partner with another individual to study and correspond by phone or e-mail.

The thematically connected hymns in each volume can be studied at any time and in any church season. The structure makes this volume especially suited for study in the season of Lent.

The material is planned for weekly gatherings. The meeting place could be at church or in homes. The key will be finding a place where everyone can feel safe as they share, reflect, and pray together.

This study is ideal for rotational leadership. As leaders and participants discover an increased connection between worship and study, their understanding of leadership will continue to broaden. If a pastor is a part of your group, include him or her in the rotation. The opportunity to operate as a participant will be welcomed.

Adults of all ages and stages will find this study useful—singles groups, men's breakfasts, mom's time out, and new member study are just a few ideas. Because of the universality of the hymns used in this series, a young adult group may be as vital as an older adult group.

Planning each session

Gathering for the story

The first three pages of each session introduce the hymn. The instructions invite you to transition from a time of fellowship as you arrive, to gathering your thoughts about the hymn, checking in with each other, then experiencing the hymn (see page 6), and finally praying together.

Learning the story

This section provides relevant information about the text, the tune, and the legends of each hymn. The intent is not in-depth study, but an opportunity to discover stories and anecdotes about the persons and circumstances that were a part of the creation of the hymn.

Our story

Hymns and songs carry emotional and cognitive memories. In this section, you will be asked to reflect on how the hymn has been part of your growth in the Christian faith. The questions, similar in all sessions, provide time and a safe opportunity to share how the music and poetry has affected who we are as believers.

The biblical story

Unless the hymn writer indicated a specific biblical passage, the intended textual connection can never be certain. The writer of this study discovered textual connections and images for one stanza of each hymn and has provided questions to help you search for personal meaning related to faith traditions and the Bible.

Texts were selected from the New Revised Standard Version of the Bible (NRSV), but each participant may use his or her own Bible. Using a variety of translations can bring new perspectives to your discussions.

Additional questions to reflect on in this section of the study are:

◆ What is normally taken for granted about this passage?

◆ What is related to your own journey of faith?

◆ What connections to biblical and doctrinal understanding do you find?

◆ What may affect you personally in this text?

Living the story

Each hymn study ends with several questions addressing how this hymn will affect the way you live your faith as a result of your learning. What message will you bring to each day?

Each session ends with praying and singing. The closing prayer (with time for individual petitions) and singing the hymn weave new dimensions to the hymn's familiar words and images.

Experiencing the hymn

An important part of this study is the experience of singing. Whether your group is large or small, raise your voices together each week. If a piano and accompanist are available, look for the full score in your favorite hymnal. Most hymns are included in *Lutheran Book of Worship* or *With One Voice*, and may be found in most traditional Christian hymnals.

If your group has instrumentalists, invite them to play with you as you sing. Perhaps someone's hidden talent will shine! Invite a young person or two from your congregation who play in their school orchestra or band to play along for one session.

Many of the hymns in the Sing the Faith volumes appear on numerous recordings. The reference list on page 47 offers a starting place for your search. You might publicize your study in your church newsletter or bulletin by listing the hymns and asking for recording recommendations. In addition, piano collections that include one or more of the hymns are suggested on this page.

Whether you sing *a cappella* or with a pipe organ at its fullest, enjoy your time with the music, with the texts, with memories of the past and hope for the future, and with each other as together you Sing the Faith.

THE GLORY OF THESE FORTY DAYS

1 The glo - ry of these for - ty days we cel - e -
2 A - lone and fast - ing Mo - ses saw the lov - ing
3 So Dan - iel trained his mys - tic sight, de - liv - ered
4 Then grant, O God, that we may, too, re - turn in

brate with songs of praise; for Christ, through whom all
God who gave the law; and to E - li - jah,
from the li - ons' might; and John, the Bride - groom's
fast and prayer to you. Our spir - its strength - en

things were made, him - self has fast - ed and has prayed.
fast - ing, came the steeds and char - i - ots of flame.
friend, be - came the her - ald of Mes - si - ah's name.
with your grace, and give us joy to see your face.

Text: Latin hymn, 11th cent.; tr. Maurice F. Bell, 1862–1947, alt.
Music: ERHALT UNS, HERR, attr. Martin Luther, 1483–1546; *Geistliche Lieder*, 1543.

GATHERING FOR THE STORY

The hymns in this study have congregational melodies that sing well in unison without instrumental accompaniment. Start with the voices of the people. Save the instruments for later. Someone should practice the hymns to lead the singing.

Have a Bible and *Lutheran Book of Worship* (LBW), *With One Voice* (WOV), or hymnals and supplements from other denominations. Materials allied to such books could be helpful, like the *Hymnal Companion to Lutheran Book of Worship, With One Voice: Reference Companion, LBW: Ministers Desk Edition* (MDE), and *Lutheran Book of Worship: Manual on the Liturgy.*

Sing the hymn, discuss the questions, and pray the prayer. *(10 minutes)*

In your experience, what is the significance of the forty days of Lent? (For the history of Lent, see sources like the LBW Manual, pages 305–306.)

How do you relate preparation for and renewal of baptismal promises to fasting and prayer in your Lenten journey?

Do you find it helpful to "celebrate with songs of praise" during Lent?

Almighty God,
  we give you thanks for those who have
  faithfully served you and the church
  by writing hymns and tunes.
Help us to learn of your grace
  through their work and to celebrate Lent
  with songs of praise;
through Jesus Christ our Lord. Amen

THE GLORY OF THESE FORTY DAYS

The glory of these forty days
we celebrate with songs of praise;
for Christ, through whom all things were made,
himself has fasted and has prayed.

Alone and fasting Moses saw
the loving God who gave the law;
and to Elijah, fasting, came
the steeds and chariots of flame.

So Daniel trained his mystic sight,
delivered from the lions' might;
and John, the Bridegroom's friend, became
the herald of Messiah's name.

Then grant, O God, that we may, too,
return in fast and prayer to you.
Our spirits strengthen with your grace,
and give us joy to see your face.

Latin hymn, 11th cent.; tr. Maurice F. Bell, 1862-1947, alt.

LEARNING THE STORY

After participants read the hymn background, talk about information they found meaningful or helpful.
(5 minutes)

Note how this hymn is organized. The first stanza introduces Lent and its songs. Christ is central to these songs because, though the world was made through him, he did not remain aloof from us. Amazingly, he came among us—fasted and prayed with us. The second and third stanzas recall the larger story of God's continual search for us that culminates in Christ. The last stanza is a prayer that we ourselves may turn to God in prayer and fasting, as Christ did, and be strengthened in our lives.

The text

The origins of hymns the church has found worth keeping are sometimes obscure, and their histories circuitous, as the church takes communal ownership of them. This Latin hymn may have originated with Gregory the Great or someone else in the sixth century. By the tenth century, the church used this hymn at morning prayer during Lent, and in the nineteenth century, Maurice Bell, a musician and clergyman at St. Mark's in London, constructed the English version. In this text the church celebrates the Lenten season as a forty-day journey of "glory," with "songs of praise" to Christ, who himself gave us an example of fasting and prayer (stanza 1).

The tune

Texts are often married to tunes from other times and places. ERHALT UNS, HERR comes from sixteenth-century Germany. Martin Luther, or whoever wrote the tune, adapted it from a popular twelfth- or thirteenth-century melody.

The legend

"Legend" often means fictitious fairytale, something untrue. In this study, "legend" refers to what a family creates when telling its story. Family members may tell the same story in different—even contradictory—ways, but the story is profoundly true. In this hymn, the "legend" names Gregory the Great as the author. Gregorian Chant is also named for Gregory. He may or may not have had much to do with either. In both cases, the church has made the text and music its own, associating them with a great figure in its history.

OUR STORY

Describe your life as a story. Who are the main characters? What role does God play?

You may need to adapt these questions for the participants in your group. Ask them to record their responses and then share their stories.
(10 minutes)

Who chooses whom in baptism and in the Christian life? Does the hymn give you any clues?

A fundamental insight of Christianity is that we are always tempted to see God in our image and to assume that what we do is the center and measure of all things. This hymn points to the Christian reversal of that temptation by affirming that God is the center and measure of all things, the center of our Lenten discipline, and of the whole Christian life. God strengthens us and gives us joy (stanza 4). Baptism, Lent, and Christian living begin, continue, and end in God.

Why is Christ the central figure here? How does God choose you?

Invite participants to find the passages in their Bibles and record responses to the questions.

After Christ's importance is established in stanza 1, four Biblical figures in stanzas 2 and 3 call to mind the huge story about God and us.

Moses, at God's bidding, delivered the people from slavery and gave the law—the commandments. Elijah fasted and proclaimed God's glory. Daniel, known to us in what is called "apocalyptic" literature, in his faithfulness was protected from lions. John the baptizer heralded the Messiah and marks baptism as a central Lenten theme. This huge sweep comes again at the end of Lent in the Easter Vigil, where the readings include Moses and the exodus and Daniel and the fiery furnace.

(For all the readings, see the MDE, pages 143–153.)

For Christ, through whom all things were made
John 1:1-18

Who was Christ? What makes him unique?

Alone and fasting Moses saw the loving God who gave the law
Exodus 19:20 and 19:25-20:17

Who was Moses? Why is he important?

And to Elijah, fasting, came the steeds and chariots of flame
1 Kings 19:4-18 and 2 Kings 2:9-12

Who was Elijah? Why does he deserve notice?

So Daniel trained his mystic sight, delivered from the lions' might
Daniel 2:19, 36 and 6:16-23

What is the book of Daniel about?

Determine if your group would prefer to:

◆ read and respond to all passages and questions before talking

◆ read, respond, and discuss one passage at a time

(20 minutes)

And John, the Bridegroom's friend, became the herald of Messiah's name
Mark 1:1-14

What did John do?

Prayer and fasting are present throughout this story (and the hymn), as they are in Lent and in the whole Christian life. But note: they can be used to escape the commandments that direct us to care for the world around us. That use is a perversion to which God responds to us as to Elijah: "What are you doing here? . . . Go." (See 1 Kings 19:9b, 13b, and 15.) That is, fast and pray; then serve your neighbor.

LIVING THE STORY

Invite participants to reflect for a few moments on today's conversation, and then respond to the questions. It is important to share the responses to these questions so your group can offer prayer support to each other throughout the week.

Select a leader for your next meeting and remind everyone of the time and location.

Close by singing "The Glory of These Forty Days" and praying together. *(10 minutes)*

The Christian life can be misunderstood as counting how many points we get for the good we do, when it's really about God, who searches us out. It can also be misunderstood as only prayer and fasting, with no care for the neighbor, when it's also about works. We get no credit for the works, but God calls us to do them.

Why should we turn in fasting and prayer to God?

Who and what strengthen our spirits?

Where does the Lenten discipline lead?

Lord Christ,
    through whom all things were made,
    you fasted and prayed on our behalf.
Grant us grace to turn in fasting and prayer
    to you, to celebrate our Lenten journey
    with songs of praise,
    and to follow you into the world.
In your name we pray. Amen

BY THE BABYLONIAN RIVERS

1 By the Bab - y - lo - nian riv - ers we sat down in grief and wept;
2 There our cap - tors in de - ri - sion did re - quire of us a song;
3 How shall we sing the . . Lord's song in a strange and bit - ter land?
4 Let the cross be ben - e - dic - tion for those bound in tyr - an - ny;

hung our harps up - on a wil - low, mourned for Zi - on when we slept.
so we sat with star - ing vi - sion, and the days were hard and long.
Can our voic - es veil the sor - row? Lord God, hold your ho - ly band.
by the pow'r of res - ur - rec - tion loose them from cap - tiv - i - ty.

Text: Ewald Bash, 1924–1994. © 1964 The American Lutheran Church, admin. Augsburg Fortress.
Music: KAS DZIEDAJA. Latvian folk tune.

GATHERING FOR THE STORY

Why is it hard for the singers to sing?

The tune of the last hymn (ERHALT UNS, HERR) is moved forward by a bold muscular push. This tune (KAS DZIEDAJA) is more plaintive and flexible, drawn forward by its end point rather than pushed from its beginning.

The tunes match their texts. The last one, about songs of praise, needs a bold musical setting. This one, about grief, holds back in lament so it can weep on the way to its goal.

Where are they?

Sing the hymn in unison again without accompaniment and led by those who have practiced it, then discuss the questions and pray the prayer.
(10 minutes)

How, Lord, can we sing your song
　　in a strange and bitter land
　　when any of us is held in captivity
　　or derided?
Yet your cross is benediction
　　for all who are tyrannized,
　　and your power of resurrection
　　breaks the bonds of all who are bound.
Grant us,
　　and all who take counsel
　　for the common good,
　　to live out your peace and freedom.
Amen

BY THE BABYLONIAN RIVERS

By the Babylonian rivers
we sat down in grief and wept;
hung our harps upon a willow,
mourned for Zion when we slept.

There our captors in derision
did require of us a song;
so we sat with staring vision,
and the days were hard and long.

How shall we sing the Lord's song
in a strange and bitter land?
Can our voices veil the sorrow?
Lord God, hold your holy band.

Let the cross be benediction
for those bound in tyranny;
by the pow'r of resurrection
loose them from captivity.

Ewald Bash, 1924–1994.
© *1964 The American Lutheran Church, admin. Augsburg Fortress.*

LEARNING THE STORY

After participants read the hymn background, talk about information they found meaningful or helpful. *(5 minutes)*

The themes of this hymn resonate with the prayer and fasting of Lent that focus on Christ's journey to the cross. Yet these themes also appear throughout the church year, throughout the Bible, and throughout our lives. They call us to solidarity with the oppressed and tyrannized, whoever and wherever they may be. We are to sing their song with them in whatever halting and broken ways we can.

This song is not easy. We are tempted to make ourselves detached superiors, to raid the treasures of the oppressed, and to pretend identification with them. Lent proposes the reverse: costly self-denial and liberation in Christ from our own captivity.

The text

The text that originally went with this Latvian folk melody asks who is singing. The answer is painful: the singers are orphans serving mean lords. They are crying out for the sun to rise, to warm them and to dry their tears. Ewald Bash wrote another text for the folk tune. Bash, a pastor at churches in Ohio and a campus minister at Ohio State University, helped bring Latvian refugees from camps in Europe. In a commentary on his text, he noted how Latvian refugees were some of the oldest victims of tyranny in the twentieth century. That suggested to him the lament of Psalm 137 on which he based his hymn.

The tune

The tune comes from a nineteenth-century arrangement of the tune, though it may well be centuries older than the arrangement. Folk tunes come out of oral traditions and may be written down at some point. They include haunting melodies like this one, often stimulated by the kind of oppression this text recounts. African-Americans under slavery and Jews throughout their history have created comparable melodies.

The legend

The horror of slavery, the terror of oppression, and the untold brutality we have inflicted on one another, though buried in unwritten chronicles, are heard in hymns like this one.

OUR STORY

Who are the captors in our day?

You may need to adapt these questions for the participants in your group. Ask them to record their responses and then share their stories.
(10 minutes)

Who is in captivity among us?

Sometimes captivity is obvious, as when Hitler put Jews in concentration camps and killed them. (The hymn tells of captors' derision and being bound in tyranny.) Sometimes it's less obvious, as when our greed exploits the poor yet is hidden from view, submerged in denial, or when we push the marginalized out of sight and treat them badly. The Christian faith calls us to be concerned about, to care for, and to liberate orphans, widows, and all those who are oppressed or abused—since we are all liberated in Christ. This is our song.

Are we in captivity? How?

Invite participants to find the passages in their Bibles and record responses to the questions.

Psalm 137 recalls the destruction of Jerusalem in 587 B.C. and the captivity in Babylon. The people were denied worship in the Temple, and their captors made matters worse by mocking them and forcing them to sing the songs they would have sung in the Temple. While we can remember this historical circumstance, we broaden the Psalms' meaning to many circumstances and to a wide use throughout the church year. This is a poignant lament that encompasses all the horrible ways we treat each other.

Which of Psalm 137's verses are used by Bash in the hymn? Why?

Let the cross be benediction for those bound in tyranny; by the pow'r of resurrection loose them from captivity
Romans 8:18-25

Why does the hymn writer add the cross and resurrection, which are not in the Psalm, to stanza 4 of the hymn? Do they belong there?

What do you make of verse 9 in the Psalm?
Is it about vengeance or expressing anger?

Determine if your group would prefer to:

◆ read and respond to all passages and questions before talking

◆ read, respond, and discuss one passage at a time

(20 minutes)

How do you handle anger about injustice, abuse, or oppression? What is the value of the psalmist's honesty before God?

By the Babylonian rivers we sat down in grief and wept

Does the hymn deal with anger, or is it about grief?

LIVING THE STORY

Invite participants to reflect for a few moments on today's conversation, and then respond to the questions. It is important to share the responses to these questions so your group can offer prayer support to each other throughout the week.

Select a leader for your next meeting and remind everyone of the time and location.

Close by singing "By the Babylonian Rivers" and praying together.
(10 minutes)

Singing hymns is a comforting but dangerous business, just like encountering Christ. Hymns embody the faith. Singing laments like Psalm 137 leads both to comfort in Christ and to solidarity with the poor and outcast. When we are among the oppressed, we receive comfort. When we can take action, we work on behalf of the oppressed.

How do you as a Christian approach oppression and related societal concerns like pollution, racial and gender justice, and war and peace?

How can the church ally itself with the work of Habitat for Humanity, Bread for the World, food closets, shelters, and rape crisis prevention agencies?

Almighty God,
 we give you thanks for folk melodies,
 for Ewald who wrote this hymn,
 and for all those who have
 "found out" musical texts and tunes.
Let them help us sing your song,
 even in a strange and bitter land;
through Jesus Christ our Lord. Amen

AH, HOLY JESUS, HOW HAVE YOU OFFENDED

1 Ah, ho - ly Je - sus, how have you of - fend - ed that mor - tal
2 Who was the guilt - y? Who brought this up - on you? A - las, my
3 Lo, the Good Shep - herd for the sheep is of - fered; the slave has
4 For me, kind Je - sus, was your in - car - na - tion, your mor - tal
5 There - fore, kind Je - sus, since I can - not pay you, I do a -

judg - ment has on you de - scend - ed? By foes de - rid - ed,
trea - son, Je - sus, has un - done you. 'Twas I, Lord Je - sus,
sin - ned, and the Son has suf - fered; for our a - tone - ment,
sor - row, and your life's ob - la - tion; your death of an - guish
dore you, and will ev - er pray you; think on your pit - y

by your own re - ject - ed, O most af - flict - ed,
I it was de - nied you; I cru - ci - fied you.
while we noth - ing heed - ed, God in - ter - ced - ed.
and your bit - ter pas - sion, for my sal - va - tion.
and your love un - swerv - ing, not my de - serv - ing.

Text: Johann Heermann, 1585–1647; tr. Robert Bridges, 1844–1930, alt. © 1994 Augsburg Fortress.
Music: HERZLIEBSTER JESU, Johann Crüger, 1598–1662.

GATHERING FOR THE STORY

Who is the "I" in this hymn? Is it you, your neighbor, the church, the world, all of the above, or none of the above? Why does it matter who the "I" is?

The next three hymns plunge us into the story of the Passion narratives, the central texts of Holy Week. Here we follow Jesus to the cross and find both our inhumanity and the staggering grace of God. That we crucified and rejected the innocent one, who rescued us anyway, is what the church and this hymn grapple with. This hymn uses the church's shorthand in words like "atone" and "intercede" to express how God in Christ stands in for us and bears our sins.

How does this hymn understand God's intercession for us? What does it mean to intercede?

Like the first two hymns, this tune sings well in unison, but it also lends itself well to four parts. Either way will work. If you sing it in parts, a quartet who has practiced could lead. (See LBW 123 for four-part accompaniment.)
(10 minutes)

When guilt and wrong
   lay us low, God, remind us
   of Jesus and the cross.
When life and its problems
   overwhelm us, teach us again
   that Jesus has taken our burdens
   on his back
and nailed them to the cross for us.
And help us to be thankful. Amen

AH, HOLY JESUS,
HOW HAVE YOU OFFENDED

Ah, holy Jesus, how have you offended,
that mortal judgment has on you descended?
By foes derided, by your own rejected,
O most afflicted.

Who was the guilty? Who brought this upon you?
Alas, my treason, Jesus, has undone you.
'Twas I, Lord Jesus, I it was denied you;
I crucified you.

Lo, the Good Shepherd for the sheep is offered;
the slave has sinned, and the Son has suffered;
for our atonement, while we nothing heeded,
God interceded.

For me, kind Jesus, was your incarnation,
your mortal sorrow and your life's oblation,
your death of anguish and your bitter passion,
for my salvation.

Therefore, kind Jesus, since I cannot pay you,
I do adore you, and will ever pray you:
think on your pity and your love unswerving,
not my deserving.

Johann Heermann, 1585–1647; tr. Robert Bridges, 1844–1930, alt.
© 1994 Augsburg Fortress.

LEARNING THE STORY

After participants read the hymn background, talk about information they found meaningful or helpful.
(5 minutes)

J. S. Bach has been called the "fifth evangelist" because, as a composer, he was one of the most faithful "preachers" of the church. In his setting of the St. Matthew Passion, he harmonized stanzas 1, 3, and 4 of this hymn's original fifteen, and in his setting of the St. John Passion, he harmonized stanzas 7, 8, and 9. These remarkable meditations on Jesus' passion and death, especially in the context of the passion narratives themselves, provide insights no words can give.

The text

Johann Heermann, a pastor in a small German town called Köben, based this hymn on a meditation of John of Fécamp, an eleventh-century monk, medical expert, and writer. John's meditations were so good they were wrongly attributed to both Augustine (354–430) and Anselm (c. 1033–1109). Robert Bridges, an English medical doctor and Poet Laureate, translated Heermann's hymn in the Yattendon Hymnal that he helped to edit at the end of the nineteenth century. This text sees Jesus as the sacrificial Lamb who "intercedes" for us by dying to pay the price of our sin—which is one way the church has understood the "atonement" or work of Christ.

The tune

The tune first appeared in 1640 with another text in one of the publications by Johann Crüger. Crüger, cantor at St. Nicholas Church in Berlin, wrote fine hymn tunes and published hymnals. This tune seems to have its roots in the Genevan Psalter melody for Psalm 23, and another melody by Johann Hermann Schein (1586–1630), who was one of the cantors in Leipzig at the St. Thomas Church prior to J.S. Bach (1685–1750).

The legend

In 1616 Heermann's town of Köben was struck by fire; in 1617 Heermann's wife died; and in 1618 the Thirty Years' War began and thereafter devastated Köben on numerous occasions. Heermann himself was the only one of his parents' five children to live. He was ill as a child, and throat problems forced him to retire in 1638. In the face of all of that, he wrote this text.

OUR STORY

Discuss whether you think the hymn writer goes too far in describing us as guilty. In what ways are we guilty, treasonous, deniers, and crucifiers of Jesus?

You may need to adapt these questions for the participants in your group. Ask them to record their responses and then share their stories.
(10 minutes)

Does the weight fall on our guilt or on God's lifting our guilt in Jesus' life and death?

It is possible to wallow in guilt in a life of sickness. Then we miss the forgiveness and love God offers in Christ that lifts the weight of guilt and yields a life of adoration in the light of Easter. This hymn points to such a healthy life. Notice how each stanza comes to the point in the final short line and makes a progression: from seeing Christ's affliction, to the realization that we crucified Jesus, to God's interceding for our salvation, to God's unswerving love in spite of what we logically deserve.

What does it mean to live a life of adoration?

THE BIBLICAL STORY

Invite participants to find the passages in their Bibles and record responses to the questions.

The writer of this hymn has taken on a cosmic scope that pulls together many threads of the Biblical narrative around Christ's sacrifice for us. The accounts of Jesus' passion and death, the suffering servant songs of Isaiah, and the analysis of Paul in Romans are all part of this scope.

Hymns like this one gather these many Biblical connections together. They function for the body of the baptized as a means to voice the Biblical faith. It's as if they say, "That's just what I wanted to express, and now I have words for it." The community of faith embraces hymns like this one long after the hymn writer is forgotten.

Read part of one of the accounts of Christ's passion and death, like Mark 15:6-15. Does the hymn reflect this account faithfully?

By foes derided, by your own rejected, O most afflicted
Isaiah 53:7

The book of Isaiah includes what have been called "servant songs," in which God's chosen one stands in for the people and is disfigured in the process. Look up part of one such song in Isaiah 53:4-9. How has the hymn writer picked up this imagery?

*Paul thinks systematically in Romans 5:6-11.
Do you recognize any of his thoughts in the
hymn?*

Determine if your
group would prefer
to:
◆ read and respond
to all passages and
questions before
talking
◆ read, respond,
and discuss one
passage at a time

(20 minutes)

*Does Heermann weave together Biblical
thought coherently? How would you do it?
What would you emphasize?*

LIVING THE STORY

Invite participants to reflect for a few moments on today's conversation, and then respond to the questions. It is important to share the responses to these questions so your group can offer prayer support to each other throughout the week.

Select a leader for your next meeting and remind everyone of the time and location.

Close by singing "Ah, Holy Jesus" and praying together.
(10 minutes)

This hymn moves from God's acting in Christ to our adoration of God, and then implies concern for the neighbor, just as the Commandments remembered in the first hymn require. There's another hymn that explicitly ties together adoration and care for the neighbor, "Lord, Thee I Love with All My Heart" (LBW 325).

What happens in your life when forgiveness is absent?

What happens in your life when forgiveness is present?

What is the relation between adoration of God and living for others?

> Lord Jesus,
>   how have you offended,
>   that we derided and rejected you?
> Yet you took on our flesh
>   and suffered death on the cross for us.
> Remember not our iniquity,
>   and help us to adore you
>   for your mercies' sake. Amen

O SACRED HEAD, NOW WOUNDED

1 O sa - cred head, now wound - ed, with grief and shame weighed down,
2 How art thou pale with an - guish, with sore a - buse and scorn;
3 What lan - guage shall I bor - row to thank thee, dear - est friend,
4 Lord, be my con - so - la - tion; shield me when I must die;

now scorn - ful - ly sur - round - ed with thorns, thine on - ly crown;
how does that vis - age lan - guish which once was bright as morn!
for this thy dy - ing sor - row, thy pit - y with - out end?
re - mind me of thy pas - sion when my last hour draws nigh.

O sa - cred head, what glo - ry, what bliss till now was thine!
Thy grief and bit - ter pas - sion were all for sin - ners' gain;
Oh, make me thine for - ev - er, and should I faint - ing be,
These eyes, new faith re - ceiv - ing, from thee shall nev - er move;

Yet, though de - spised and gor - y, I joy to call thee mine.
mine, mine was the trans - gres - sion, but thine the dead - ly pain.
Lord, let me nev - er, nev - er out - live my love to thee.
for he who dies be - liev - ing dies safe - ly in thy love.

Text: Paul Gerhardt, 1607–1676, based on Arnulf of Louvain, c. 1250; tr. composite.
Music: HERZLICH TUT MICH VERLANGEN, German melody, c. 1500, adapt. Hans L. Hassler, 1564–1612.

GATHERING FOR THE STORY

The very first line of this hymn addresses the "sacred head." Does that seem unusual to you? Who is being addressed? Why does the hymn writer speak in this fashion? (You might want to look up the word synecdoche *in a dictionary.)*

"O Sacred Head" is a meditation about Jesus on the cross. The "intercessory" theme of the last hymn is here (in the line, "Mine, mine was the transgression, but thine the deadly pain," for example), but that theme is folded into another one. This hymn starts with Jesus on the cross and then turns to our thanks and the benefits we receive.

Many poems of this sort are individual meditative expressions that remain individual. This one, perhaps because it affords a communal yet personal identification with Christ and his death, has captured the imagination of the church as a whole and has found expression in its common worship.

(10 minutes)

In the first line of the third stanza, language is "to be borrowed." What is the point of such a thought?

Almighty God,
    we search for words to sing
    of your passion and death.
Give us language
    to meditate on your cross
    so that with faithful consolation,
    we may have new eyes for seeing
    and new ears for hearing;
through Jesus Christ, our Lord,
    to whom with you and the Holy Spirit
be glory forever. Amen

O SACRED HEAD, NOW WOUNDED

O sacred head, now wounded,
with grief and shame weighed down,
now scornfully surrounded
with thorns, thine only crown;
O sacred head, what glory,
what bliss till now was thine!
Yet, though despised and gory,
I joy to call thee mine.

How art thou pale with anguish,
with sore abuse and scorn;
how does that visage languish
which once was bright as morn!
Thy grief and bitter passion
were all for sinners' gain;
mine, mine was the transgression,
but thine the deadly pain.

What language shall I borrow
to thank thee, dearest friend,
for this thy dying sorrow,
thy pity without end?
Oh, make me thine forever,
and should I fainting be,
Lord, let me never, never
outlive my love to thee.

Lord, be my consolation;
shield me when I must die;
remind me of thy passion
when my last hour draws nigh.
These eyes, new faith receiving,
from thee shall never move;
for he who dies believing
dies safely in thy love.

Paul Gerhardt, 1607-1676, based on Arnulf of Louvain, c. 1250; tr. composite.

LEARNING THE STORY

After participants read the hymn background, talk about information they found meaningful or helpful.
(5 minutes)

The Latin text, a prayerful meditation called "Salve mundi salutare," has been ascribed to Bernard of Clairvaux. He was a powerful force in the twelfth century, but a person of prayer as well. He felt the geometric proportion of churches was good for the sound of prayer, but he wasn't too fond of visual decoration. More recently, Arnulf von Loewen (c. 1200–1250) has been proposed as the author, but nobody knows for sure who wrote the text.

The text

The Latin poem on which this hymn is based has seven sections, each section addressed to a part of Christ's body on the cross. Paul Gerhardt, one of the most important Lutheran hymn writers, cast the whole poem into German. The portion addressed to the head of Christ was used in the 1656 edition of Johann Crüger's *Praxis Pietatis Melica*, the major German hymnal of the seventeenth century. From there, text and tune spread throughout the church. James Waddell Alexander, a nineteenth-century professor at Princeton Seminary and pastor of Fifth Avenue Presbyterian Church in New York City, largely made this English translation.

The tune

This tune, by the Lutheran church musician Hans Leo Hassler, was first published in 1601 in its rhythmic version (LBW 116) to go with a love song, an acrostic to a woman named Maria. In 1613 the funeral text "Herzlich tut mich verlangen" joined the melody and named it. Then, in Crüger's Praxis, the original German version of "O Sacred Head" was used with this tune. That move gave the tune its other name, PASSION CHORALE.

The legend

J.S. Bach made this melody central to his setting of the St. Matthew Passion. He harmonized it for five stanzas of "O Sacred Head" and one stanza of a different hymn. The pitch sinks each time the tune recurs. The last time an active final chord comes is just before the temple curtain is rent in two.

OUR STORY

If you were to write a meditation like this hymn, what would it say?

You may need to adapt these questions for the participants in your group. Ask them to record their responses and then share their stories.
(10 minutes)

Why has this devotional meditation seized the imagination of the church for so long? Perhaps its poetry and content account for its presence in so many hymnals and translations because they give the baptized words to identify with Christ on the cross.

"O Sacred Head" is a product of the twelfth or thirteenth, seventeenth, and nineteenth centuries, from Latin, German, and American English sources. How does the hymn reflect its times? How might our times lead to different images? What sort of images?

Perhaps the tune's quality and durability has helped to keep the text in play. The tune certainly has had an interesting life. First used for a love song, then for a funeral hymn, then as the PASSION CHORALE, Paul Simon recently employed it for his "American Tune" after Art Garfunkel introduced it to him via one of Bach's harmonizations.

THE BIBLICAL STORY

Invite participants to find the passages in their Bibles and record responses to the questions.

There is for most Christian people an inevitable devotional side to their faith. Most Christians cannot express their devotion the way good poets can, however, so they gravitate to words that wordsmiths make for them. This is a good thing.

But there is a danger. If the devotion of the person takes center stage and becomes the measure of all things, the first commandment has been broken. Our self-centeredness takes over, and we try to make ourselves into God.

The Bible is about what God in Christ does for us. Once we realize that, of course we will think, meditate, write, and sing about it.

O sacred head now wounded, with grief and shame weighed down

Do you assume a devotional attitude when you read the Passion narratives in the Bible?

Yet, though despised and gory, I joy to call thee mine

If so, would you express your attitude the way this hymn does? If not, what kind of response would you make?

Can too close a scrutiny of the suffering of Jesus be unhealthy? What makes such a scrutiny healthy?

Determine if your group would prefer to:

◆ read and respond to all passages and questions before talking

◆ read, respond, and discuss one passage at a time

(20 minutes)

Does the hymn accurately portray what the Bible says, as in Matthew 27:29-30?

LIVING THE STORY

Invite participants to reflect for a few moments on today's conversation, and then respond to the questions. It is important to share the responses to these questions so your group can offer prayer support to each other through-out the week.

Select a leader for your next meeting and remind every-one of the time and location.

Close by singing "O Sacred Head" and praying together. *(10 minutes)*

As finite creatures, we are concerned about dying. Christians don't side-step this concern, but they live in the knowledge that death is a reality. It cannot be avoided the way much of current culture tries to pretend. We die as whole creatures— bodies, minds, and spirits. But death is not the final word. We die safely in God's love in Christ.

What does this hymn ask about our dying? How would you paraphrase the request?

Does the hymn relate our dying to Christ's dying? How?

Does the imagery about outliving our love to Christ play into the imagery about dying? How?

God, in Christ
    you have borne the sin of the world.
    We have no words to thank you.
When we come to die, remind us
    that you enfold us in your love
    in the Passion of your Son,
in whose name we pray. Amen

SING, MY TONGUE

1 Sing, my tongue, the glo - rious bat - tle; sing the end - ing
2 Tell how, when at length the full - ness of the ap - point - ed
3 Thus, with thir - ty years ac - com - plished, he went forth from
4 Faith - ful cross, true sign of tri - umph, be for all the
5 Un - to God be praise and glo - ry; to the Fa - ther

of the fray. Now a - bove the cross, the troph - y,
time was come, he, the Word, was born of wom - an,
Naz - a - reth, des - tined, ded - i - cat - ed, will - ing,
no - blest tree; none in fo - liage, none in blos - som,
and the Son, to the e - ter - nal Spir - it hon - or

sound the loud tri - um - phant lay; tell how Christ, the
left for us his Fa - ther's home, blazed the path of
did his work, and met his death; like a lamb he
none in fruit your e - qual be; sym - bol of the
now and ev - er - more be done; praise and glo - ry

world's re - deem - er, as a vic - tim won the day.
true o - be - dience, shone as light a - midst the gloom.
hum - bly yield - ed on the cross his dy - ing breath.
world's re - demp - tion, for your bur - den makes us free.
in the high - est, while the time - less a - ges run.

Text: Venatius Honorius Fortunatus, 530–609; tr. John M. Neale, 1818–1866, alt.
Music: FORTUNATUS NEW, Carl F. Schalk, b. 1929. © 1967 Concordia Publishing House. Used with permission. All rights reserved.

GATHERING FOR THE STORY

Do you regard life as a battle? If so, what are you battling?

You may want to ponder this hymn slowly and encourage other members of the class to do the same. It can be understood relatively quickly at one level, but you may find deeper meaning with longer and more thoughtful contemplation. Someone might read the poetry aloud before the class sings the hymn together.

The tune given here is from the twentieth century. You can also sing the hymn to its more traditional chant tune, PANGE LINGUA (LBW 120). Either tune works well in unison. If you sing the text to both tunes, you might ask whether they highlight different aspects of the text or even suggest different meanings. *(10 minutes)*

This hymn suggests that God fights on our behalf and that Christ as victim wins the day. What might that mean?

In the midst of the struggles of our life,
  God, give us and all the baptized
  the wisdom and will to fight the forces
  that seek to destroy us and our world.
Loose our tongues to sing
  the victory Christ has won.
In Christ, with Christ, and through Christ,
  all honor and glory be to you
  and the Spirit while timeless ages run.
Amen

SING, MY TONGUE

Sing, my tongue, the glorious battle;
sing the ending of the fray.
Now above the cross, the trophy,
sound the loud triumphant lay;
tell how Christ, the world's redeemer,
as a victim won the day.

Tell how, when at length the fullness
of the appointed time was come,
he, the Word, was born of woman,
left for us his Father's home,
blazed the path of true obedience,
shone as light amidst the gloom.

Thus, with thirty years accomplished,
he went forth from Nazareth,
destined, dedicated, willing,
did his work, and met his death;
like a lamb he humbly yielded
on the cross his dying breath.

Faithful cross, true sign of triumph,
be for all the noblest tree;
none in foliage, none in blossom,
none in fruit your equal be;
symbol of the world's redemption,
for your burden makes us free.

Unto God be praise and glory;
to the Father and the Son,
to the eternal Spirit honor
now and evermore be done;
praise and glory in the highest,
while the timeless ages run.

Venantius Honorius Fortunatus, 530-609; tr. John M. Neale, 1818-1866, alt.

LEARNING THE STORY

After participants read the hymn background, talk about information they found meaningful or helpful.
(5 minutes)

Venantius Fortunatus was born in Northern Italy and became the bishop of Poithiers. He wrote both humorous little rhymes for his friends at dinner parties and great hymns for the church. This hymn, though written for a specific procession, transcended its origins. It was appointed for use from Passion (or Palm) Sunday through Wednesday of Holy Week, and for Good Friday. It is now used more generally in Lent and Holy Week.

John Mason Neale (1818–1866), an Anglican priest and linguist who did remarkable and faithful service in an obscure place called East Grinstead near London, made the English version.

The text

The last two hymns viewed Christ's "work" as interceding for us, standing in for us as a sacrificial "lamb." That imagery was developed more fully after this hymn was composed. "Sing, My Tongue" expresses the thought of the early church that saw a struggle between God and death. Death was even personified and "thought" that by killing Christ it would win the battle. But the tables were turned, and death itself was killed. Luther used this idea in "Christ Jesus Lay in Death's Strong Bands" (LBW 134) where we sing that death swallows up death.

The tune

The tune is by Carl Schalk, one of the twentieth century's leading American Lutheran church musicians and writers. Named for Fortunatus, the text's likely author, Schalk's tune is more rhythmic and robust than the chant tune associated with this text (LBW 120). The chant tune is named PANGE LINGUA for the opening Latin line of the hymn. In the LBW, PANGE LINGUA is paired with a famous text by Thomas Aquinas, "Of the Glorious Body Telling," which in Latin also begins with "Pange lingua."

The legend

Venantius Fortunatus (c. 530–609) is generally credited with composing the Latin original of this hymn, though some have thought the fifth-century theologian and chant leader Claudianus Mamertus wrote it. The usual view is that Fortunatus intended it for a procession of a relic of the cross that his friend Queen Radegund had procured for the convent of St. Croix, which she founded in Pothiers.

OUR STORY

What is the battle and "the ending of the fray" that the writer of this hymn refers to?

You may need to adapt these questions for the participants in your group. Ask them to record their responses and then share their stories.
(10 minutes)

A typical scenario for us goes like this: the hero with right on his or her side slays the evil person and saves the day. The Christian church poses an alternative that goes like this: the God of heaven and earth in Christ submits to the cross and redeems us; that is, Christ as victim wins the day.

What is meant by the tree? How does the writer explore that image?

The church tells a hard truth here. Only in the fictional world of the movies does righteous violence "win." In life there is no righteous violence. Violence is always tainted by evil, and it always begets more violence. Only in Christ's cross is the battle won.

Why do we sing in response to Christ's victory?

THE BIBLICAL STORY

Invite participants to find the passages in their Bibles and record responses to the questions.

J.S. Bach interpreted the work of Christ sacrificially in his St. Matthew Passion, much like the hymns "Ah, Holy Jesus" and "O Sacred Head, Now Wounded." In his setting of the St. John Passion, he interpreted Christ's work as defeating sin and death, more like "Sing, My Tongue." Bach was aware of the way the two evangelists told the story of Jesus and how they reflected different emphases. He was faithful to these varying understandings of what God has done in Christ. His example suggests that there is wisdom for us in singing hymns that, in their differences, reflect the fullness of the story.

Tell how Christ, the world's redeemer, as a victim won the day

Read Matthew 26:1-5 and John 18:1-11. How do these two introductions to the Passion narratives set up what is to come?

What differences do you see?

How do the two evangelists view Jesus?

Determine if your group would prefer to:
◆ read and respond to all passages and questions before talking
◆ read, respond, and discuss one passage at a time

(20 minutes)

What is the same about these accounts? What is different?

LIVING THE STORY

Invite participants to reflect for a few moments on today's conversation, and then respond to the questions. It is important to share the responses to these questions so your group can offer prayer support to each other throughout the week.

Since this is the last session, take a few minutes to talk about future study this group might want to pursue.

Close by singing "Sing, My Tongue," or you may wish to sing all five hymns from *Hymns of Lent*. End the session by praying together. *(10 minutes)*

Christ both stands in for us in our guilt and wins the battle over sin and death; freeing us to live for others: first, in personal relationships with our neighbors; and second, in the laws and structures of our society.

What does it mean that only in Christ's cross is the battle won? Are there times when, while still taking into account our own evil, we nonetheless have to do violence to oppose evil? How dangerous is that? How wise?

Are there implications for conflicts like the one between the Israelis and the Palestinians? What are they? How would you work to resolve such conflicts?

God of all that was, is, and will be,
  in Christ's death, sin and death
  have been destroyed,
  and our freedom is won.
Give us lives to live the cross and its victory
  in praise to you,
  who with the Son and the Spirit
lives and reigns forever. Amen

RESOURCES

Compact Discs

J.S. Bach, *St. John Passion*, BWV 245 ("Ah, Holy Jesus," stanza 7, track 3; stanzas 8 and 9, track 17). Smithsonian Chamber Players and Chorus, Kenneth Slowik, conductor. Smithsonian Collection of Recordings, 1990, CD ND 0381.

Johann Sebastian Bach, *St. Matthew Passion*, BWV 244 ("Ah, Holy Jesus": stanza 1, track 1:3 (Nr. 3); stanza 3, track 1:19 (Nr. 19); Stanza 4, track 2:11 (Nr. 46); HERZLICH TUT MICH VERLANGEN with "O Sacred Head": stanza 5, track 1:15 (Nr. 15); stanza 6, track 1:17 (Nr. 17); with Befiehl du deine Wege, track 2:9 (Nr. 44); with "O Sacred Head," stanzas 1 and 2, track 2:19 (Nr. 54); stanza 9, track 2:27 (Nr. 62). Gabrieli Players, Paul McCreesh, director. Deutsche Grammophon, CD 474 200-2.